Almost Mrs.

wedding date

Writing my Love Story

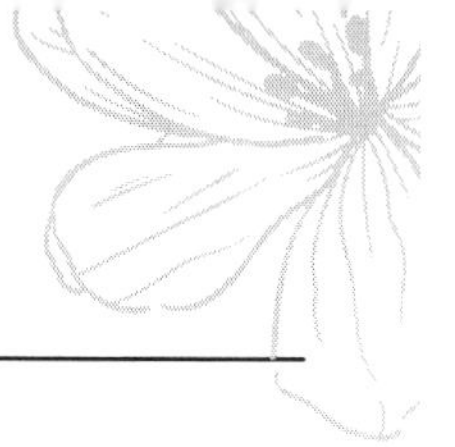

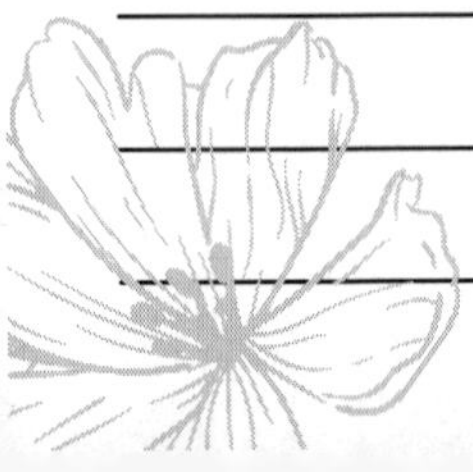

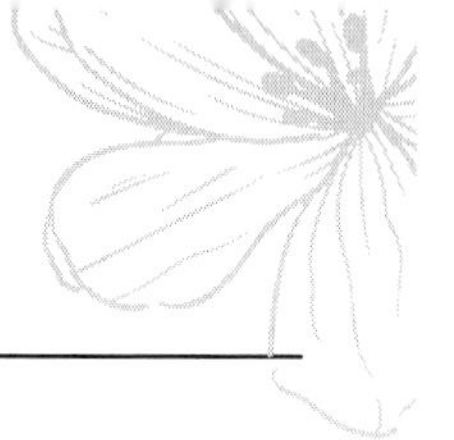

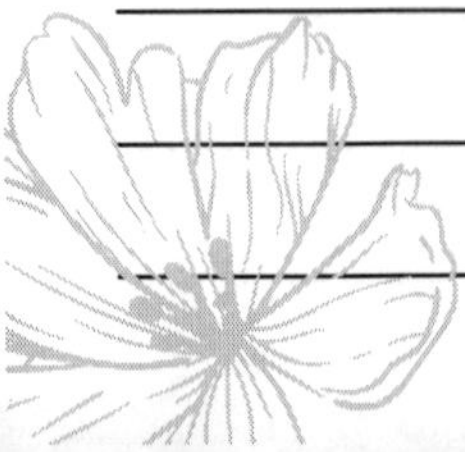

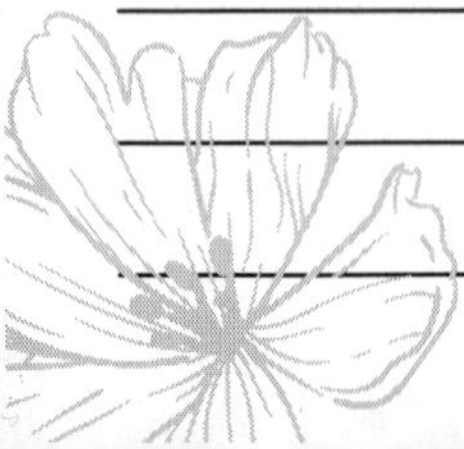

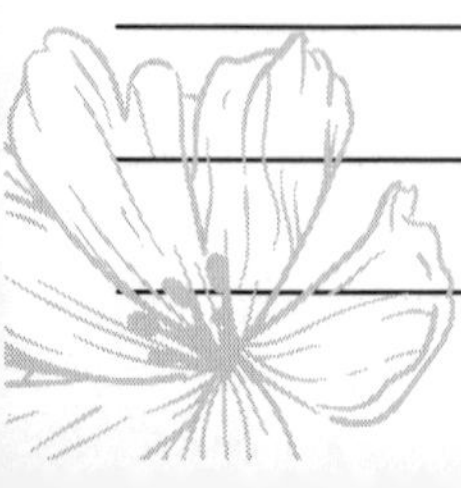

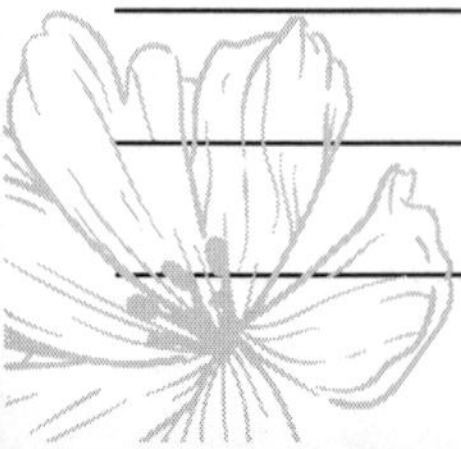

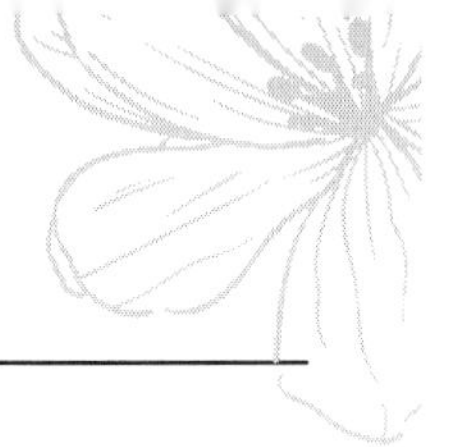

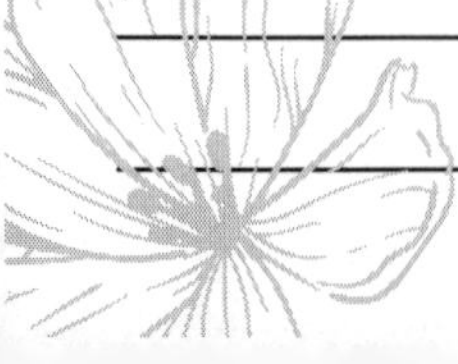

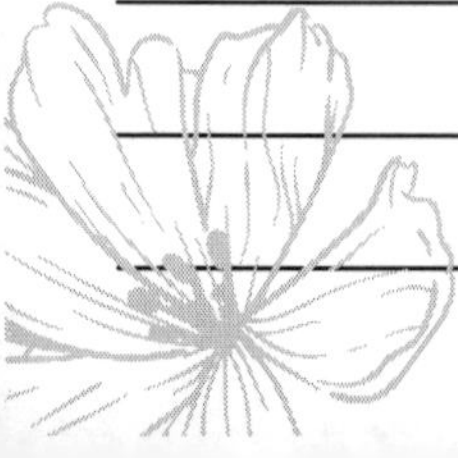

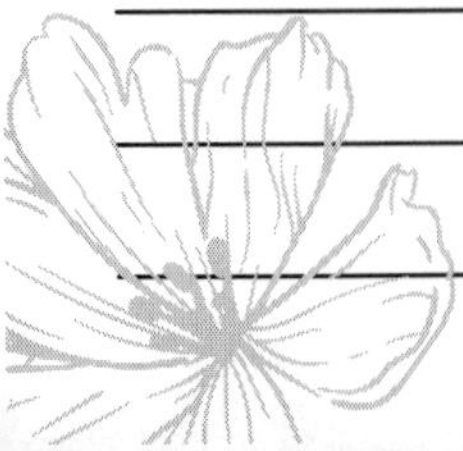

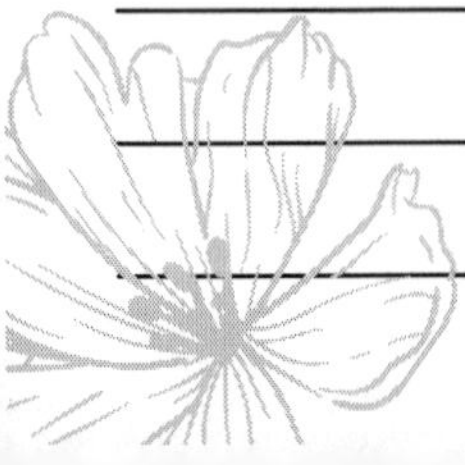

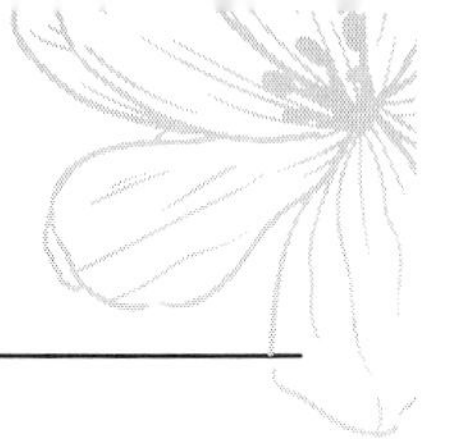

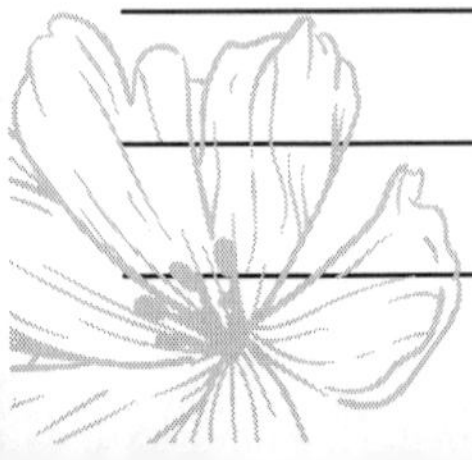

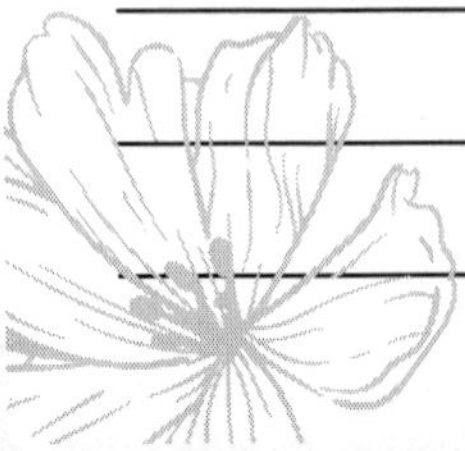

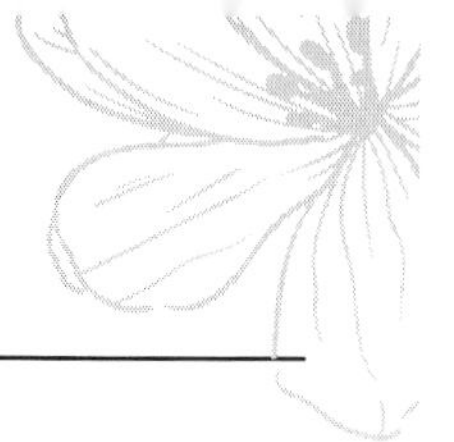

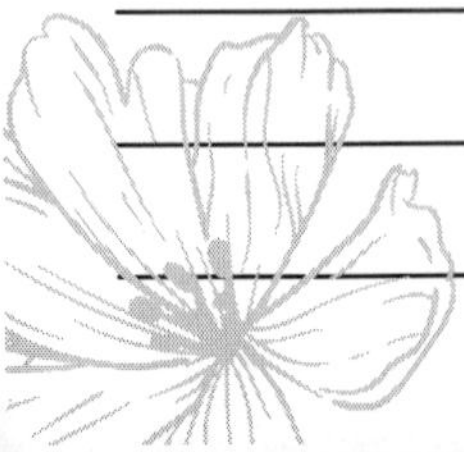

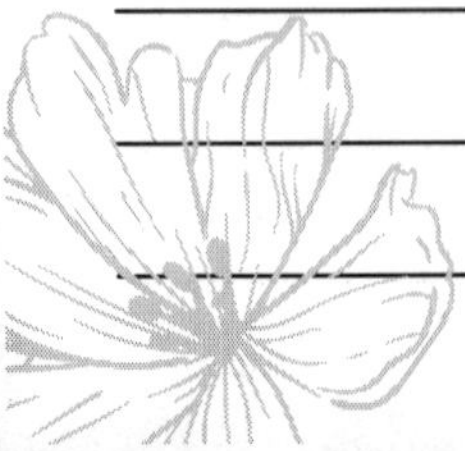

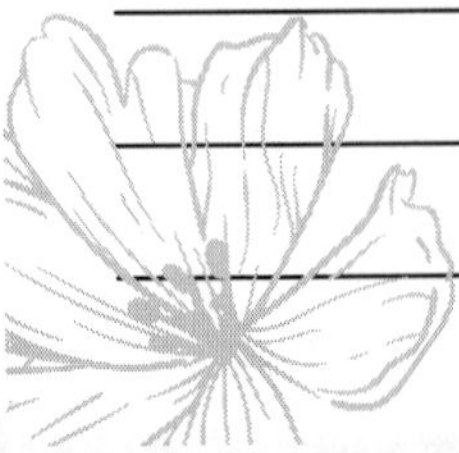

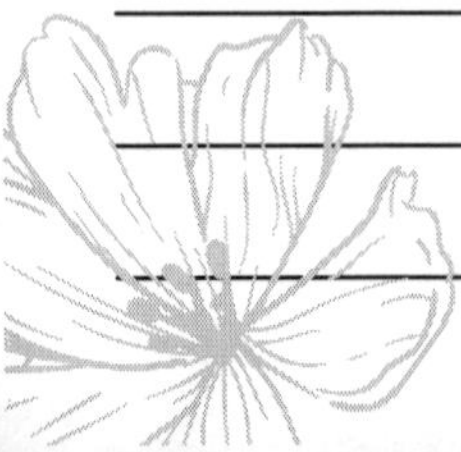

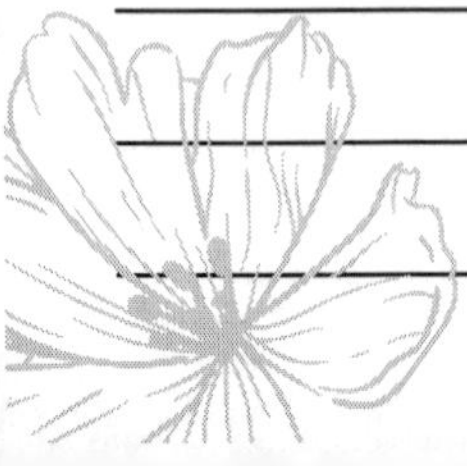

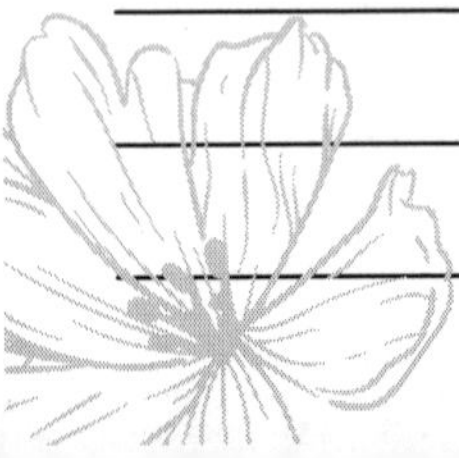

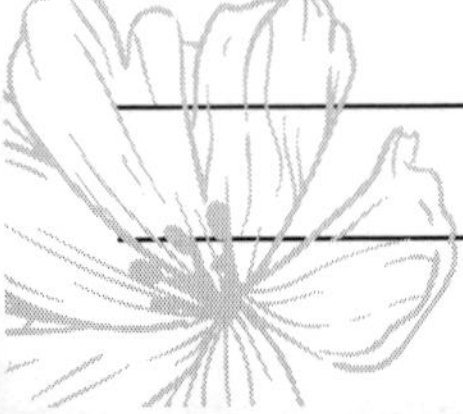

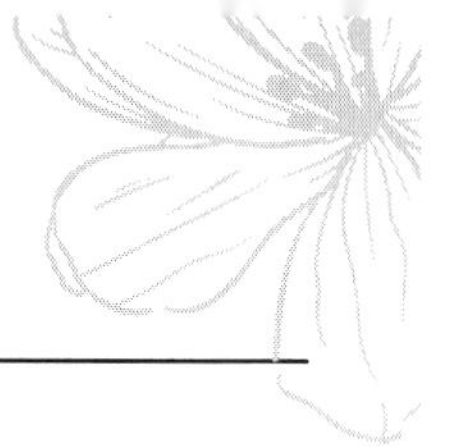

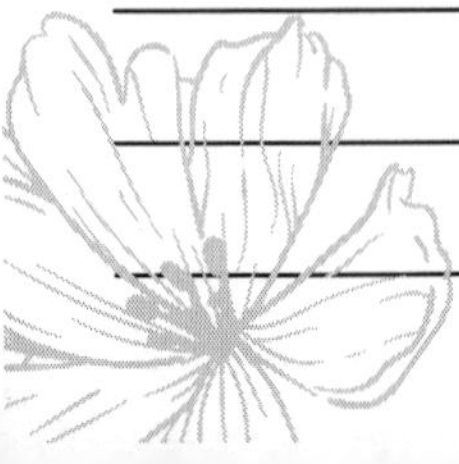

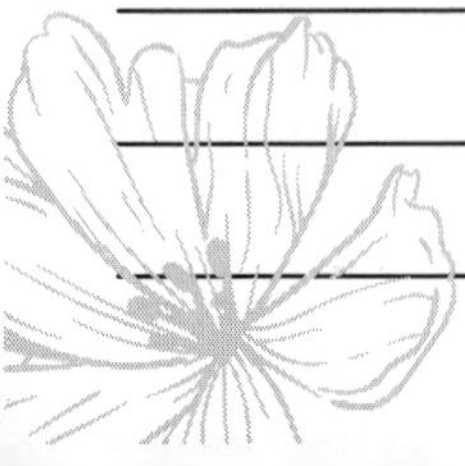

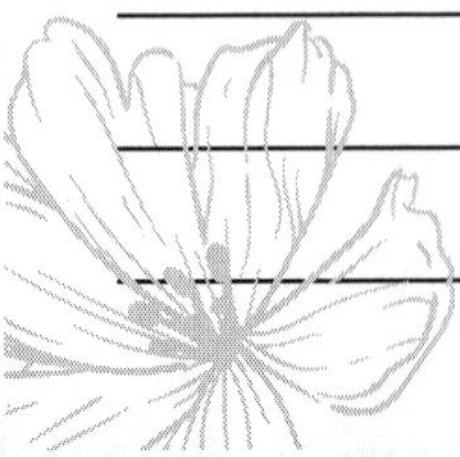

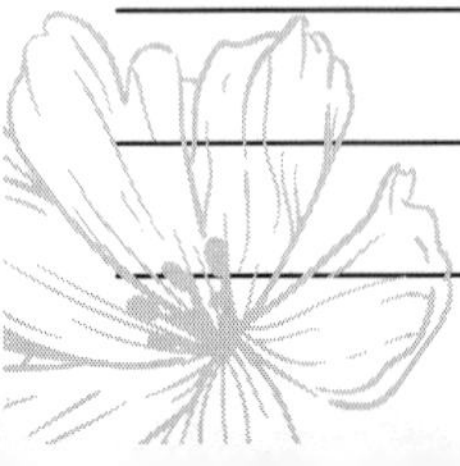

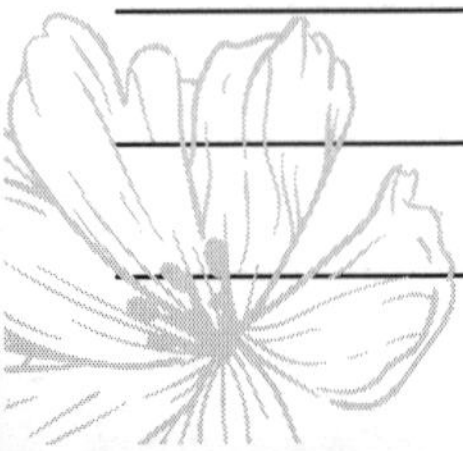

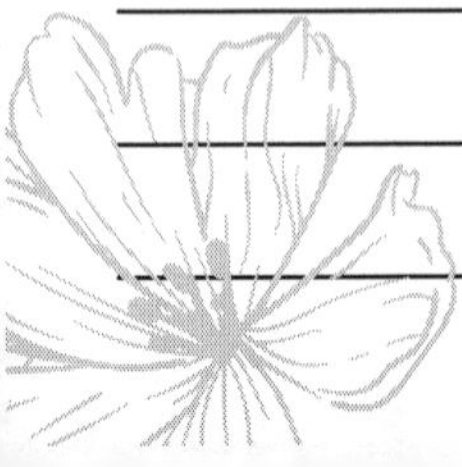

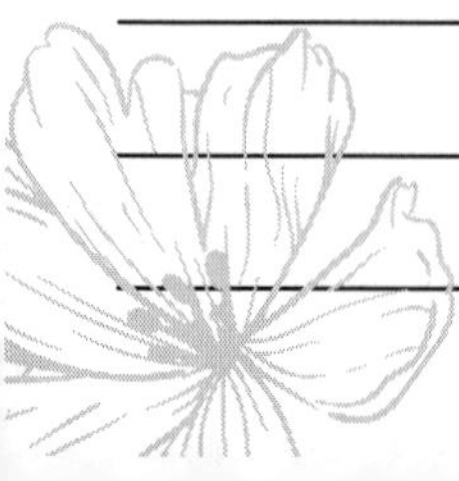

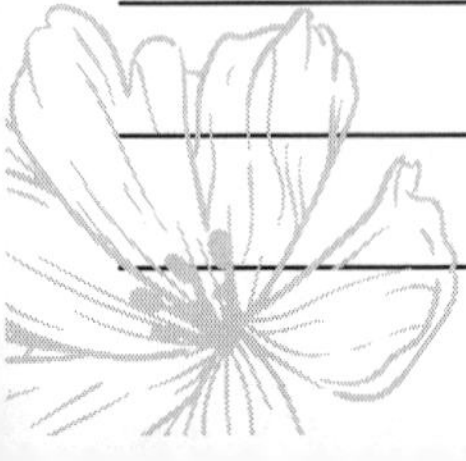

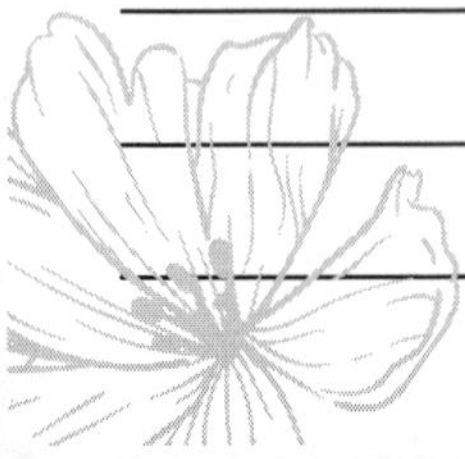

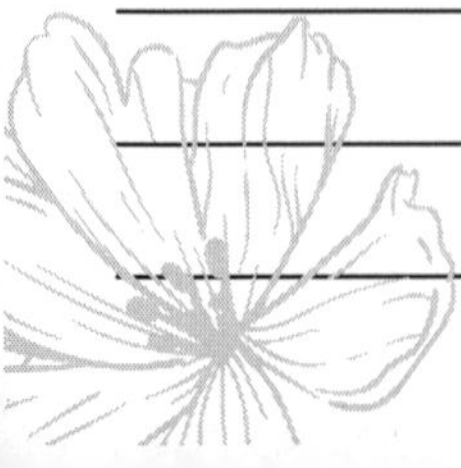

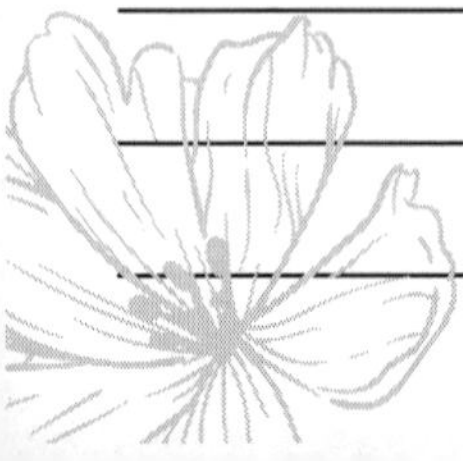

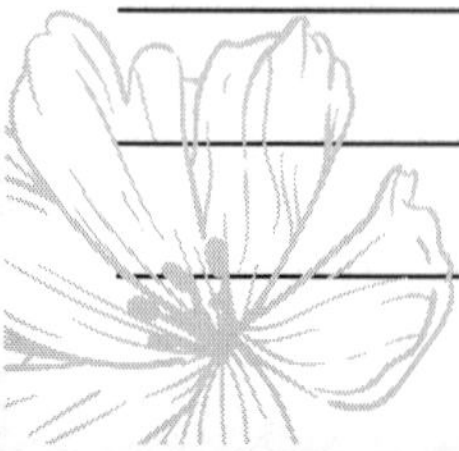

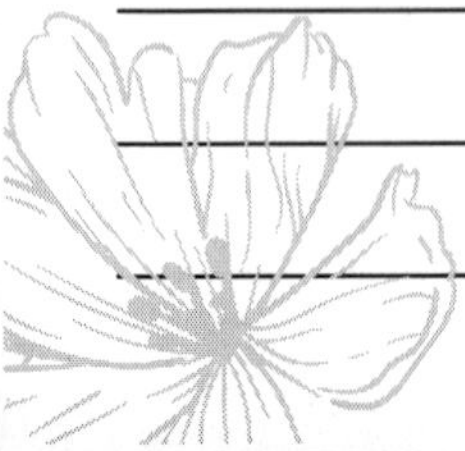

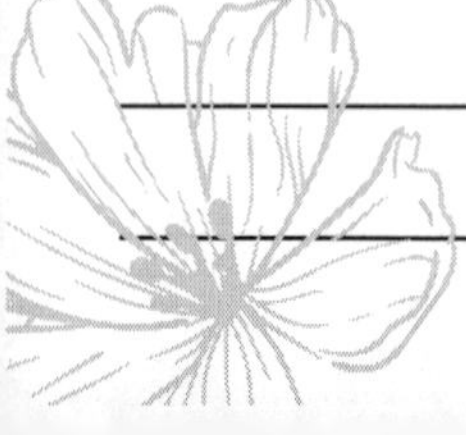

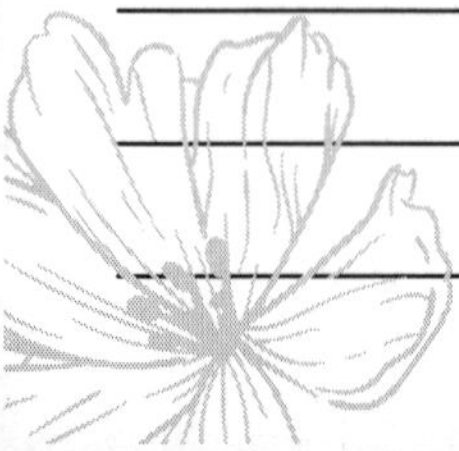

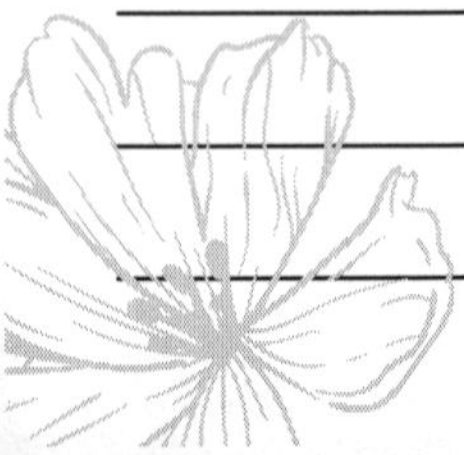

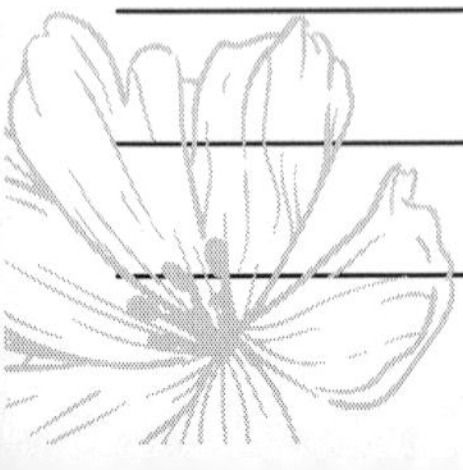

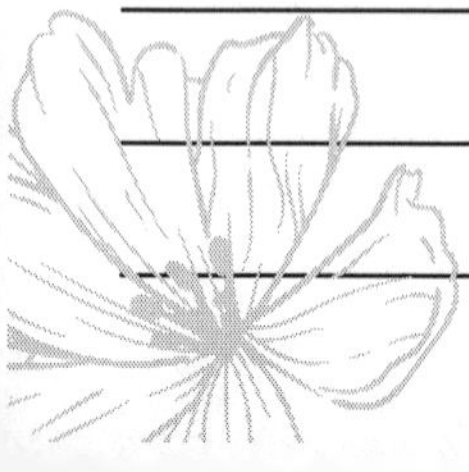

Made in the USA
Middletown, DE
02 May 2023

29899420R00061